Money Manners for Kids

How to Teach the Next Generation about Finances

Sandra C. Bartell

All rights reserved.

This book or no parts of this book may be reproduced, transmitted in any form or by any means electronic, mechanical, photocopy, recording or otherwise without written permission from the author.

Copyright 2016

First published in Greensboro, North Carolina

Printed in the United States of America   2016

Cover design: Ashley D. Hill

ISBN: 978-0-9899947-4-3

I dedicate this book to my grandparents and parents. They were instrumental in my life, encouraging me to learn good work ethics and help others in need. They both instilled in me pride in doing a job well done.

My maternal grandparents lived near us so I visited them almost every day. My grandfather, Roy always had a bag of treats for me. He called me "Sandy Andy Candy." My grandmother, Gertrude could cook delicious food. She worked at home, raising her family. Later in life, she worked for a family with young children. She went to work every day despite rain, sun or snow. My grandfather was an entrepreneur. He built a workshop, grew his garden and had all kinds of fruit trees and grapevines. He made hair pomade (grease) and printed his own labels. He also made furniture and peppermint candy. He even sent a letter to a furniture company in New York about his furniture. Later, he worked at our local school as a janitor.

My paternal grandparents also were instrumental in my life. My grandmother transitioned before I was born but I saw pictures and I fell in love with her and her name, Queen Esther! I call myself Queen. My grandfather, Roosevelt was a pastor so he instilled high morals in us, work ethics and being true to who we were created to be.

My parents, Edward and Virginia had great work ethics also. They both could be counted on to do their jobs. My dad is 88-years-old and encouraging his grandchildren to do well in life. He encouraged them to go to college since he only had a fourth grade education. It didn't stop him from driving a truck delivering furniture, planting a garden, fruit trees and grapevines. My mother had an 11th grade education and had beautiful penmanship. She learned and recited poems like *"In the Morning"* by Paul Lawrence

Dunbar. She enjoyed baking, making jellies, cakes, pies and giving them away.

They both cleaned our home church at no cost and bought products out of their own money. They believed in leaving an inheritance for their children's children.

Acknowledgements

I would like to thank Mae and Jim Murray for encouraging me to write this book. I thank Jim for his services providing research, additional writing and editing for the manuscript. I also thank My Econ Team for the knowledge I have gained since becoming an Executive Vice President as well as our pastor, Michael Thomas for teaching us how to be good stewards and the rest of my family and friends for their prayers.

Thanks to my husband Victor, who has been with me through every adventure I've been on. As a beautician, teacher, Girl Scout Leader and other various jobs, he always was there by my side. I thank him for the times I was away, even if we were in the same room.

I'm grateful to my teachers, especially my fifth and sixth grade teacher, Mrs. Kiser. She was a classy lady in all her ways and modeled how to be a professional and classy at the same time.

We taught our girls and the Girl Scouts how to raise money for many trips to places like New York, Washington, DC, Georgia, Florida and South Carolina. We wanted to expose our daughters and other daughters to a different world than their back yard and change their mindsets.

Thanks to our daughters, Victoria and Sonya, who are educators and are very dedicated to their careers and are valuable assets in their profession. We talk all the time about students and how we can motivate them to do their very best. They always tell me, "Mom, this is your time. Go for it!"

So, here I go ladies! Thanks for helping me stay focused and true to who I am.

My grandson, Dominique, the joy of my life. I call him my grandbaby (really? – a 24-year-old, 6'4" handsome young man). He enjoys family and calls us often to see how we are doing. He also has compassion for others, works with youth at a nonprofit organization and always has words of encouragement and scriptures from the Bible for me.

I thank my son-in-law, Gerald for his famous words: "Hey, my mama!" As an educator (athletic director), he gives me words of encouragement as well as challenging questions for me to ponder.

Foreword

By Jesse Gathewright

Sandra Bartell is a wonderful individual and an awesome educator. She is well-respected in the community and in the education arena.

I was excited and honored that she asked me to write a foreword in her new book.

I believe that this book will make a significant difference in the life of parents as well as young readers as they gain the financial literacy and education that they need.

Financial education is a unique subject that requires specialized expertise to teach effectively. The quality of financial education through this book can directly influence both short-term student outcomes and long-term impact on their financial well-being.

Teaching your children about money with this book will help them discover the relationships between earning, spending and saving. In doing this, children also begin to understand the value of money. This financial literacy book can begin at a young age with simple money concepts such as counting coins and make change for purchases. Older children can learn about savings accounts, balancing a checkbook and creating a personal budget.

Teaching children about financial literacy through this book is very important if you want them to grow up to be financially responsible adults. Kids will take a greater interest in financial literacy if the topic is engaging and fun. However, nothing is more important than making open money conversations a regular part of their daily life and upbringing as they grow into adulthood.

(Jesse Gathewright is the founder of Financial Destiny, Inc., a non-profit agency devoted to increasing the financial skills of individuals and families, and purposed to decrease the financial stress that can lead to sub-prime living. Since its inception, Financial Destiny, Inc. has worked and is actively working with numerous clients, youth and various non-profit agencies to further address the need for financial literacy and education).

Additional Endorsements

Congratulations to my wife, Sandra, for writing her first of many books. This has been on her bucket list for quite a while now. She has retired from Guilford County School System where she worked as an elementary teacher for over 31 years – a job she really loved. She was very passionate about making sure every student would have the opportunity to be successful in the classroom.

Writing this book will help young people understand the value of money and how it works. It does not surprise me to see that she is still making contributions to the education of our young people even in her retirement years. Through this work, she will continue to ensure that young people will become successful in life. "Write On, One Million!"

Your husband of 44 years, Victor L. Bartell

I'm so proud of my mother for pursuing one of her dreams and seeing it come to fruition. She has inspired me and others to be the best God has created us to be. I know you will enjoy this book and learn the importance of saving money and being blessed at the same time.

Love, Victoria Bartell

I was not surprised when my mother shared that she would write a book about finances. She has always been a giver of money. With as much as she's giving away, I guess she decided to offer some advice and wisdom on the necessity of money. This started out as a children's book but slowly and with careful attention begin to transition into a book with talking points to share with children about the use of money. It is a "must have" for parents working to raise their children to be great money managers. This book is an easy, friendly read so parents can communicate and benefit from the practical advice and activities.

My mother continues to be an asset to her community, beginning a neighborhood tutorial service for students struggling with reading and math. She has now transitioned into teaching parents how to support their children academically and socially – by writing this book on money manners. I am so proud to be Sandra Cheek Bartell's daughter.
Sonya Bartell Herbert

This comprehensive book, designed to start the child early in financial development has proven to be perfectly complete and clear in every detail. The modern-day parent who models the "entrepreneurial" skills effective for optimal finance training sets the mold for an indelible impression upon the welded-minded child. Sandra has certainly made Money Manners the required forum for financial etiquette to be supreme and necessary for success in future endeavors, no matter what the pursuit.
Evelyn Cheek

Introduction

Manners are a method, a style, or a way of being. Manners show that someone has a good home upbringing. I believe that manners extend beyond the traditional ways we think children should behave. That's why I am writing this book.

Money Manners for Kids is from the heart of God-given wisdom to me while I was learning about finances. I had been working for over 53 years, starting as a babysitter when I was 12-years-old. I also worked in tobacco (yes, I got up early with my brothers, boarded the back of a pickup truck and went to the tobacco barn, ironing when my mom couldn't go).

I also helped clean my elementary school with my mom and of course, I worked around the house. Sometimes, it was for no pay and other times, it was for a little pay.

No matter what the returns, I came away with a great work ethic: being on time, staying on the job, giving 100 percent. Those attributes still work. They open the door for you to go back if you ever leave or get a good reference if you leave for good.

While growing up, I heard, "Money doesn't grow on trees," "Don't spend it all in one place" or "Save for a rainy day."

Let's fast-forward to the year I retired as a public school teacher. I had earned over $1 million. But how much of it did I still have? That was a million dollar question. I did not realize that now was my "rainy day."

I had received a lump sum, saved some money and invested some. However, I love shopping and entertaining so I did plenty of both. I had heard a sermon about three men who were given talents (to responsibly care for and invest). One received five talents, another received two and another one. There was a lesson to be learned about how they used what had been entrusted to them. I soon realized that I was guilty of having the one talent. Where was all that money I made in my career? What happened to it?

As a retiree, I cannot go back and start over. But going forward will be different. It was very important for me to change my mindset. Money is not just for spending!

I have dedicated most of my adult life teaching young children. Starting with the acronym SMART (Saving Money Always Requires Teaching), my goal for this book is to jumpstart a discussion that has been too lacking in too many homes. This book will provide a resource for those parents who are concerned enough to have an on-going dialogue with their children about financial responsibility.

I will share insights with families on how children will benefit from proven strategies and home-based training on money and finances in an ever-changing world.

Financial literacy is obviously one of the most important topics parents can share to ensure that their children are prepared to succeed in "the real world." This easy-to-read book provides essential details and a plan to answer the question: will my child be ready to handle finances successfully as an adult?

I have included a special chapter with references to the Bible since it is not only a book of spiritual guidance but has practical wisdom as well.

I am writing this book to help.

Table of Contents

Chapter 1- Who's Job Is This? 1

Chapter 2 - How to Get the Ball Rolling 3

Chapter 3 - When Should You Start? 5

Chapter 4 -Questions About Money 7

Chapter 5 - Basic Training: Sandra's Teachable Moments 13

Chapter 6 - Saving Options 15

Chapter 7 - Insurance Considerations 19

Chapter 8 - Investing for the Future 21

Chapter 9 - Wisdom from the Bible 23

Glossary - 30

Words from the Author - 34

Chapter 1

Whose Job Is This?

Let me be clear about this.

Parents: you should be your children's most trusted advisers. Work to build that trust at the earliest stages of their lives. They should be comfortable coming to you with questions about anything and everything.

One of the greatest gifts parents can give their children is the benefit of their knowledge and wisdom. Financial issues should be at the top of the list. If you want your children to stand out as a model for others, teach them everything you can about how to handle money!

Many adults never had formal training on financial planning. If they did, it was not in the home. They may have watched their parents' successes and failures. And then they made their own mistakes along the way. They owe it to their children to set a firm foundation that will follow them for the rest of their lives.

These are some basics that go along with this teaching that will help children have a responsible attitude about the connection between money and overall good stewardship. Your values and character should be reflected in your children.

A Work Ethic Should Begin In the Home

Teach children:

- To be respectful of all adults
- To respond when they are called
- To say "please" and "thank you"
- How to start picking up their toys
- How to clean their eating space
- How to pick up and hang up clothes
- How to make their bed and clean up their room
- That their clothes and toys will last longer if they are cared for

- Children should be taught the biblical admonition that "it is better to give than to receive." Charity should begin in the home. Sometimes sharing within a household is a difficult concept to learn, but the benefits are wonderful to see in action. As they grow out of clothing items and toys, teach them to donate what they don't want to keep to the Salvation Army, Goodwill or other consignment shops or local thrift stores.

Chapter 2
How to Get the Ball Rolling

If you're determined to focus on your children's financial literacy and you're committed to working with them, here are some tips to organize yourself before you begin. Whether you have one child or more than one of different ages, it's vital to have a plan before you start.

Here is a checklist of topics to consider:

- What are you doing to continue your own financial education?

- Would you benefit from having a financial planner to help you gain sound fiscal advice?
- Are you keeping up with technological advances allowing banking and investing on IPhones and other handheld devices?

- How is life different for your children than when you were going up?

- What is your child or children's aptitude on financial issues?

- What do you feel are the most important issues to emphasize?

- What is your policy on giving your child or children an allowance?

- What plans for saving money do you have for your child?

- When should I start saving for college if I believe my child is on that path?

- What are age-appropriate chores I can assign to my children?

- How do I feel about using cash as a performance incentive and a reward for good grades (ie: honor roll)?

- How will I respond when my child expects me to buy something I cannot afford?

- How can I make this training fun and engaging?
- Am I willing to sacrifice some of my wants to fulfill my child or children's needs?

Chapter 3

When Should You Start?

Children need to be trained on the wisdom of how to handle money. I have compiled strategies for parents to begin teaching their children before the day they enter elementary school.

Children will spend more time at home than anywhere else, especially in their younger years. It is generally considered that training on financial issues should begin between the ages of 3 and 5.

A plan needs to be in place beginning at the earliest age. That's when kids watch our every move. Starting with trips to the mall or grocery store, young children observe how the exchange of money brings rewards. They watch with fascination as parents surrender cash or a plastic card in stores and get merchandise. Their card and even cash is returned by the clerk.

Children are impressionable and parents should be on alert to peer pressure and the challenges that other children may make. If the lifestyle and values of their friends are different than your household, you will need to show them how and why there is a difference. For instance, if that friend lives in a very materialistic home and gets whatever he or she wants, they may cause your child to envy that attitude.

And while not starting out at this young age, parents with older children should start nevertheless. By the time they reach middle school, another phase of training should begin. When they become teenagers, the final phase of training before leaving home should kick in.

The following chapters contain questions that can facilitate the basis for conversations and actual training.

Chapter 4
Questions about Money

Many adults need to change their mindsets about money. Too many of us have not learned the wisdom of budgeting, planning and spending wisely. And that results in not setting good examples for our children.

In the face of today's turbulent economic times, the American Dream is still a goal for every generation: to secure a great job, buy a home and at least one car, get married and start a family, raise children to adulthood, vacation as desired and secure a comfortable retirement. The theme of this book is: if you have money, you can have exciting experiences. Money will help create those experiences. Traditionally, parents want their children to live a more fruitful life than they have lived. That will only happen if they invest time and resources in Money Manners for their kids.

Why Do We Need Money?

There is a saying that nothing in life is free. Just about anything that you can look at, feel or touch costs money. It may not be able to buy happiness and other intangibles but money can help to make a difference in a satisfied life.

In order to have financial stability, lifestyle choices and financial freedom, children must learn the importance of money. We use money to buy material things and pay for the use of resources. We need money to ensure that we have a productive lifestyle while living on earth. Then, we need energy. And everything costs money. It may cost a little, it may cost a lot but it will cost something to live here.

For children, cost begins at school. Bringing money for school lunch, field trips, school pictures and school uniforms starts early. There are charitable drives (bringing in pennies for health causes and programs like The Make-A-Wish Foundation) as well as book drives.

As children go to middle school and high school, there will be overnight and weekend trips and band instrument rentals. Yearbooks and prom expenses will be added. Due to budget cuts, some schools even require students to purchase their own sports and cheerleading uniforms.

What is Money Used For?

Parents: do you remember ever hearing your mother or father say, "Money does not grow on trees." Why did they say that? Perhaps, you asked for a toy, a game, shoes, etc. and they did not have the money at that time.

Now it is your turn to deal with your children's requests. Have you ever met anyone who doesn't like to buy stuff? One of the more challenging tasks is to teach children the difference between needs and wants.

Children should understand that parents will not always buy them everything they want when they want it. They should be told that money is not limitless and there will be times when they will have to forgo or wait for what they want.

Perhaps as challenging children on how to save, it is equally important to teach them how and when to spend what they earn. When your children get their own money, either from allowances, gifts or getting a job, you should tell them to save some, spend some and give some. Also, put some in a bank. That's probably not the order of priority in most young minds.

But this message must be hammered home on a regular basis. Do NOT always spend!

Teach your child that it's okay to buy but within reason. They should make sure that they need it and not just want it. Help them to have a named account for what they want to buy: my toy account, Christmas account or shoes account. Then, they should work toward saving for that item rather than getting money and then spending it for something that is not on their named account list.

Help Them Make a Plan

- Set a goal (ie: buying a gift for a friend)
- Write the vision. I want to buy a (what) for (who) by (date)
- Set a date to begin saving
- What will you do to get the money? (chores, helping others)
- Stress that there are times they will need to be patient

If you offer to "loan" them funds to make a purchase and they promise to "pay you back," use this as a lesson on teaching them how to pay their debts on time. For instance, if they ask for $1.00 to buy a school lunch and mom or dad only has a $5 bill, they are expected to bring the change back that day.

How do you earn money?

You get a job and work! Then, you get paid. That's the most accepted way to earn.

Well, it goes a lot deeper than that (which will come later in a chapter on investing). You can buy stocks, bonds and other instruments but you must have money to do that. So, let's start at the beginning. In biblical days, money was either cattle or other possessions that were traded in a system called bartering.

Over time, money became the most accepted form of exchange. (Now, there is talk that we may be moving towards a cash-less society).

As children grow up, they should understand that while parents have bought everything they needed while they were young, that they should now begin to work and contribute towards some of the items they desire.

They should also understand that when they have their own money, they should be willing to help pay for cards or gifts to their parents, family members and friends (celebrating birthdays or other occasions).

Your child can earn money having jobs around the house or helping outside families like grandparents, aunts and uncles and even neighbors. The best way to make this work is to assign age appropriate chores to your child and model good work ethics to them.

Kristen May, writing in the *eHow* website, said, "Children can earn money without even leaving their homes if their parents have odd jobs that they are willing to pay their children to complete. Potential jobs include vacuuming, cleaning the kitchen, washing the car, babysitting younger siblings, washing the windows, raking leaves in the yard and shoveling snow."

She adds: "Responsible children can find jobs taking care of other people or animals. For example, if a neighbor with cats is going out of town, a child could visit the cats every day to feed them and clean their litter boxes. Another idea is to walk people's dogs in the afternoon so they do not have to do this chore after work. Children who are at least 10-years-old could work as a mother's helper taking care of younger children while the mother is around. By the time they are 12-years-old, some are responsible enough to work as babysitters."

Some parents reward their children for outstanding achievements such as getting on the honor role at school.

They will also receive financial gifts on birthdays, Christmas and graduations or other special occasions.

Model for your child how to become an entrepreneur. Explain the word. Show them your business or how to start their own like a lemonade stand. They will need instructions on how to begin. Let them tell you what they would like to do. Work with them to write the plan and set a date. Gather materials. Who will the consumers be? This will help them to become disciplined as they grow.

A Responsible Salesperson

Children will be called upon to participate in school-based or community-based fundraisers (ie: selling Girl Scout cookies)

They need to be trained on how to approach people they know as well as strangers.

They need to understand that everyone will not support their cause and buy their product.

They need to show good manners and say thank you to everyone – regardless of the outcome.

Remember: we are teaching them "Money Manners!"

A Warning about Overwhelming Debt

By the time children reach their teens, they can begin to do some of their own banking. They can have checking accounts with debit cards and some saving accounts that allow them to make withdrawals on their own. As they enter college, they need to understand how out-of-control spending can lead to misery.

There is peril in accumulating overwhelming debt. It's easy to get there and not easy to get out.

Many college students (and eventually their parents) have been taken aback by massive bills from credit card companies who flooded campuses with "free" and enticing card offers. When unsuspecting students, who signed up for cards without their parents' knowledge, maxed out those cards, they entered the world of negative credit reporting before graduation and their first job.

On the other hand, many other young people who have opted for a military career and enlisted have wasted their monthly earnings. Receiving a monthly paycheck for the first time, they often spent it within a day. They become the prey of unscrupulous car dealers and pawn shops, anxious to take advantage of their reckless spending habits.

Chapter 5

Basic Training: Sandra's Teachable Moments

Teachable moments happen every time a child decides he wants his parents to buy something. It could be a toy, clothing or any number of technology devices like a play station, a cell phone or an IPod. That would be an excellent time to have a conversation with that child about money. In addition:

- Show your toddler coins and teach him/her how to count money;
- Buy your child their first piggy bank (or other home bank) and help them come up with a plan to make regular "deposits";
- Take your child grocery shopping and show the difference between generic and pricier name brand labels;
- Take your child to the bank or other financial institution to open a savings account;
- Take your child to a restaurant and point out the advantage of using the children's menu;
- Show your child the difference in cost of DIY home maintenance/improvement projects as opposed to hiring a professional (ie: cutting the grass, etc.);

- Show your child the benefit of energy savings (turning off lights and devices when not in use);
- Help your child understand that leftovers and food left to spoil can add up to money wasted over time;
- Show your child that good maintenance of home and car (changing oil, rotating tires, etc.) can result in avoiding expensive repairs;
- Instruct your child on how to prepare for their first job interview;
- Teach your child the benefits of safety training for pets to save expensive vet bills;
- Show your child how to shop online if that is something you use;
- Show your child how to coupon shop if you do that;
- Show your child how you pay household bills;
- Explain the necessity of budgeting and the discipline it requires;
- Show your children how to keep receipts and detailed records of the spending;
- When your children are mature enough, tell them about retail policies like refunds, rebates and warranties.

Chapter 6

Saving Options

There is a difference between saving and investing. Both are important and necessary.

We'll look at saving in this chapter. Parents should be saving for their children. As they mature, children should be taught to begin saving as well.

Some parents purchase children banks as gifts for their infants. In fact, Target advertises 101 baby banks with some designs based on cartoon characters and sports teams.

As soon as they are old enough to understand the concept, children should be encouraged to put their money in three separate jars/banks/boxes so they will be able to see what they have saved. Some new banks are clear and even keep track of coin "deposits" as they are made and display the total amount in the bank.

Parents should consider opening an account at a local bank or credit union for their child. They may start by speaking to a bank officer at the branch where they have an account.

According to the *Netmums* website, the following are options for saving:

Instant Access Accounts: you don't need large amounts to open this account that offers flexibility for the account holders. They will be issued with a card that will allow them to withdraw money.

Fixed Rate Accounts: an interest bearing account offers a fixed rate that remains the same for years. Interest can be paid monthly or annually. Some banks offer bonuses if you reach a certain amount.

Trusts: the parent pays money which is then managed by someone who invests the money on the child's behalf. You can choose to build it up until the child reaches teenage years or sell the investment at any time.

Savings & Investments (including Junior ISAs): These are run by the government and offer a tax-free way to save through a mix of premium bonds, ISAs and savings certificates.

Children's Savings Bonds: These bonds are tax-free which means any interest they earn will be entirely untouchable. Bonds must be originally purchased by an adult and can be cashed in when the child reaches 21.

ISAs: Individual savings accounts are available as cash savings or investments in stocks & shares in businesses.

Stakeholder pensions: this is a government backed plan that allows parents to put away funds each year on their child's behalf.

Saving For College

Parents who feel that there is at least a possibility of their child or children going to college should start saving right away. It's never too early to open a savings account or set up an education savings plan that will have years to grow.

Parents of toddlers would be shocked if they researched college costs today. Statistics from the U.S. Department of Agriculture state that the average cost to raise a child in 2015 was $245,000. By the time today's children start the application process, who knows what the costs will be? In fact, another survey says that average parents will spend $1.1 million to get a child through undergraduate studies.

(A recent estimate from the College Board projects college costs in 2028 to range from $257,113 for four years at an in-state university to $524,547 for four years at a private college).

There are many options for parents to begin a college fund – even when their children are infants.

For instance, check out a 529 savings plan.

According to Carrie Schwab-Pomerantz, President of the Charles Schwab Foundation: "When it comes to keeping up with the increasing cost of higher education, a tax-advantaged college savings account such as a 529 plan is probably your best choice. This is a state-sponsored program that allows parents, relatives and friends to invest for a child's college education—making it easy for grandparents to chip in, too. Minimums for opening vary by state, but can be as low as $25. Plus, you can set up an automatic investment plan—say $50 or $100 a month—making it easy for you to keep contributing."

Other facts:
- While most plans are sponsored by individual states, you can use accumulated money at a college anywhere in the country.
- The account is tax-deferred and you won't end up paying federal income tax on withdrawals, neither on what you contributed nor the earnings.

- Most plans let you accumulate up to several hundred thousand dollars for the beneficiary.
- You can change the beneficiary to another eligible family member, and if the money goes unused, it reverts to the account holder.
- Most plans offer investment possibilities that won't eat up a lot of time.
- The plan is unlikely to limit the student's access to need-based grants, scholarships or loans.
- Some states offer state income tax deductions for 529 contributions.

Chapter 7

Insurance Considerations

Besides the obvious necessity to keep current on family health insurance (as well as regularly scheduled visits to the doctor and dentist), parents should look to purchase life insurance – not only for themselves, but their children as well.

We all believe that children will have their entire life in front of them. While that is true, a life insurance policy is not only just coverage for an untimely death. It's an investment that should not be overlooked.

Financial Advisor Brian Frederick writes in the *Nerdwallet* website: "I'm a big advocate of purchase life insurance on your children...The prudent, responsible thing is to always carry enough coverage for a child's funeral expenses.

A second big reason to buy a policy on a child is to lock in future insurability. Once a life insurance policy is underwritten and put in force, it will stay in force regardless of changes in your child's medical condition...The younger you are typically, the better your health is. By buying life insurance on a child, you won't have to worry about the following items:

- Developing an adverse medical condition that makes coverage more expensive, if it doesn't render the child uninsurable.
- Drug or tobacco use. Tobacco won't render you uninsurable in most cases. It will double the rates you pay.
- Avocation factors such as being a private pilot or extreme sports.
- Family history.
- Most people in their 20's won't buy life insurance no matter what…The best time to buy life insurance is long before you need it. The problem is that most people in their twenties think that they are invincible and usually wait to buy a policy until their 30's when they start having families and appreciate their own mortality a little more."

For instance, Gerber Life Insurance Company has a "Grow-Up Plan" which provides protection for children from infancy until to age 18. There are other benefits as well. Here are a few highlights:

- This plan provides whole life benefits that never expire and build cash value over time. The longer you keep the policy, the more cash value you build.
- And that money can be accessed as long as premiums are paid. Any healthy child 14 days old through age 14 is eligible. No health exam is necessary. Parents, grandparents and legal guardians may apply with policies starting at $5,000 up to $50,000.
- The policy automatically doubles during the year the child reaches the age of 18 and can be returned for the full cash value at the time of cancellation.
- "Child-like" premiums never increase.
- The plan guarantees future insurability.

Chapter 8

Investing for the Future

People invest for long-term financial savings – that rainy day. I will explain.

The benefit of investing is reflected in the growth of money when it is left alone for a period of time. There is a rate of return of money if they are patient and not touch the money until a certain date.

First, determine what you need the money for: (ie: retirement).

Then, set a goal and when you would like to reach that goal (ie: by age 70)

How long do you estimate it will take to reach that goal? (5 years, 10 years, 30 years)

You must know how much time you are willing to do without those funds. Generally, you are placing your trust in an individual or firm to make the decisions on where the funds will be invested.

Money market accounts – Interest bearing accounts that typically pay a higher interest rate than a savings account and provide the account holder with limited check-writing ability. It offers the holder benefits typical of both savings and checking accounts.

Mutual Funds – An investment vehicle made up of a pool of funds collected from many investors for the purpose of investing in securities such as stocks, bonds, money market instruments and similar assets.

Stocks – part ownership in a company which must be left for the long haul (ie: 25-30 years) or until retirement, if you are young. If you are older, you will need to decide what you are willing to risk.

Stock –Dividends – a sum of money paid regularly (typically quarterly) by a company to its shareholders out of its profits or reserves.

Growth investments – you can get more money in return than what you invested.

Bonds – you give $1,000 and in a term of years, you can get a percentage plus a return of your $1,000 (if it does well). They are also called income investments because they produce income.

For a newcomer to investing, it is advisable to consult a financial advisor or professional (perhaps where you bank) before making any decision on investing. There are risks in committing funds to one of these programs.

Chapter 9

Wisdom from the Bible

Many 21st century churches have financial training programs for their members. While it may come as a surprise to some, the Bible is a resource for those who are seeking wisdom on finances. For anyone who chooses to read it, there is an abundance of practical guidance. In fact, the word money is mentioned 139 times in the scriptures. (*Strong's Exhaustive Concordance of the Bible*).

God knows that we need money and He will (does) supply all of our needs. How does that happen? Money does not rain down from Heaven! God gives everyone the ability to earn a livelihood. Christians do not take their health for granted, which allows them to go to work and earn a living. The second benefit, which is not limited to believers, are the God-given skills and intellect to do a job to the best of their ability. Of course, that knowledge can be enhanced by education and on-the-job training. Those benefits are blessings not to be taken for granted.

Finally, successful financial planning requires making the right decisions and the right choices. Success or disaster can be the final result. And Bible-believing Christians will certainly pray for supernatural guidance before every major decision they make about their money.

Here are a few examples of relevant scriptures:

According to Philippians 4:19: *"But my God shall supply all your need according to his riches in glory by Christ Jesus."*

The Apostle John wrote in 3 John 2: *"Beloved, I wish above all things that thou mayest prosper and be in health, even as thy soul prospereth..."*

"But thou shalt remember the Lord thy God; for it is he that giveth power to get wealth..." Deuteronomy 8:18a

"Wherefore, if God so clothe the grass of the field, which today is, and tomorrow is cast into the oven, shall he not much more clothe you, O ye of little faith?" Matthew 6:30

However, many people work very hard for years for the wrong reasons. In Proverbs 23:6a: the scripture admonishes us to *"Labor not to be rich..."*

One of the most familiar scriptures about money is found in 1 Timothy 6:10: *"For the love of money is the root of all evil: which while some coveted after, they have erred from the faith, and pierced themselves through with many sorrows."*

Our church has been taught that the greatest investment anyone can make is in the Kingdom of God. In addition to practical tips, I will explain what it means to be in a three financial circumstances:

A Land of Lack – not having sufficient funds to meet basic needs (debts exceed income)

A Land of Even – having just enough to barely meet needs

A Land of Abundance – having sufficient funds to meet needs and having extra

I believe children should be encouraged to give an offering like their parents when they go to church.

Part of that teaching includes what I have learned by observing the 10/10/80 plan:

- Always paying tithes (10 percent) of your income to the church where you are a member;
- Always paying yourself (putting 10 percent) in your personal savings;
- Budgeting the remaining 80 percent for living expenses including bills.

- Show children an example by receiving a one dollar bill and what to do with it.
- 10 cents – tithe/giving
- 10 cents – savings (personal)
- 80 cents – live out of it with a budget

The Bible also deals with how parents should plan for the future. Among other admonitions, King Solomon writes in Proverbs 13:22: *"A wise man leaveth an inheritance to his children's children…"*

Budget Worksheet
(Sample)

Date	Income: Paycheck Amount	Expenses: Bills	Balance Remaining

10/10/80 Chart

Tithes	Personal Savings	Living Expenses

Goals Sheet
(Sample)

Goal:
Write It/Post It:
Date For Completion:

What to do After Getting the Money:	

Jobs Chart
(Sample)

Date	Hirer	Job Description	Date Completed	Amount Paid

Glossary

Account – a financial relationship an individual has with a bank or lender such as checking, savings or credit card accounts.

Annuity – a product offered by an insurance company or employer that one makes contributions immediately or later and begins receiving payments for a fixed payments or the recipient's lifetime.

Assets – items of value you own such as property and vehicles that can be converted to cash.

Balance – how much money you have or owe in an account.

Bankruptcy – when an individual is legally declared bankrupt and their assets and financial affairs are administered by an appointed trustee.

Borrow – securing cash or funds from a lending institution with an agreement to pay back the amount loaned plus interest.

Budget – a listing of planned revenue and expenditure for a given period with limits you place on spending so that you reach your financial goals.

Capital – wealth in the form of money or property.

Cash – money available on demand including currency, coins and money in savings or debit accounts.

Credit – a lending term used when a customer purchases a good or service with the agreement to pay at a later date.

Credit history – a report detailing an individual's past credit arrangements that is often sought by a lender when assessing a loan application.

Credit limit – a dollar amount that cannot be exceeded on a credit card or the maximum lending amount offered on a loan.

Credit score – a numerical value used to forecast how likely you are to pay back your debt.

Debts – money you owe someone else, most likely a financial institution such as bills, loan repayments and income tax.

Default – a failure to pay a loan or other debt obligation.

Discount – a reduction applied to the full priced of a good or service.

Dividends - an individual share in a pro rata distribution of profits to shareholders.

Equity – the value of ownership interest in a home or other property.

Gross income – the total money earned by a business before expenses are deducted.

Insurance – a contract between a client and provider with payments called premiums to cover loss of property or damage or other specifically named or described risks.

Interest – the cost of borrowing money on a loan or earned on an interest-bearing account.

Investments – financial instruments you buy with the hope that your money will grow in the future.

Liquid Asset – an asset that can be converted quickly into cash.

Loan – a finance agreement where money is borrowed from a lender and the borrower then pays it back in installments (plus interest) within a specified period of time.

Net income – how much of your income you keep after paying your bills.

Net worth – a measurement of your financial standing: what's left of your assets after you subtract your debts.

Paycheck – a regularly scheduled payment to an employee or contract worker for services rendered to fulfill a guaranteed annual salary.

Principal – the original amount borrowed on a loan or the remainder of the original amount that is still owed.

Rebate – a partial credit on the sale price of an item after purchase has been made, often administered by mailing in proof of purchase.

Receipt – a document provided to a customer to confirm payment and to confirm a good or service has been received.

Refinance – when a new loan is taken out to pay off an existing one, often to extend the original loan over a longer period of time, reduce fees or interest, switch banks or move from a fixed loan to variable loan.

Repossess – the process of a bank or other lender taking ownership of property to pay off a loan in default.

Taxes – deductions employers make from individual paychecks to cover federal and state (and sometimes local) payroll taxes. Also, sales taxes added to the cost of goods and services at the point of purchase.

Transaction – a financial event that causes money to go into or out of an account such as a charge placed on a credit card.

Warranty – a written guarantee of the integrity of a product and of the maker's responsibility for the repair or replacement of defective parts.

Words from the Author

I became a classroom teacher at the age of 33. Prior to that, I was a cosmetologist. That word is seldom used today.

I knew I wanted to teach when I was in the 8th grade. Well, life happened. Fast forward to 1983. I knew that I had found the career I wanted to retire in. Teaching was and is my calling.

I knew I also wanted to write a book and now it has finally come to fruition. I did not know what it would be about, but I knew there would be a book with Sandra C. Bartell on a bookshelf or in a bookstore. I told my first graders in 1986 to look for my book one day. WOW!

I prayed and talked to God about it all the time.

I have numerous journals and notebooks with a lot of writings. Since I retired, I have enjoyed the days of being retired. I realized the money I had accumulated was okay but I wanted more than okay.

My sister-in-law invited me to a briefing on how to minimize taxes, eliminate debt, increase cash flow and create wealth by investing. I knew I was onto something. When I finally created the quiet and listened to that still small voice, I heard, "Sandra, what do you have in your hand? Educator."

So, this book will help educate children of all ages to enjoy the life God wants for us. My husband, Victor has been that silent partner that I needed to keep me focused. He is very quiet, listens more than he talks. But when he speaks, like E.F. Hutton, everyone listens. He listens with his heart and has kept us out of financial problems. We sowed during the lean times as well as fat times. And because of that, we are reaping the benefits of our labor. We are entering into the rest and blessings of God.

Additional Resources

Websites

www.investopedia.com - Teaching Financial Literacy to Kids

www.TheMint.org – Fun Financial Literacy Activities for Kids

www.smartmoneysmartkids.com/New - class

www.Jump$tartCoalition – How to Raise a Money Smart Child

www.FinancialLiteracyforKids: A Nerd Wallet Q&A

https://corporate.troweprice.com: Money…Kids/Site

http://blog.taxact.com: The Secret of Teaching Financial Literacy to Kids